THE A–Z OF COCKTAILS

Commissioning Editor Rose Hewlett
Words by Sophie Berry
Illustrations and Design by Zoë Horn Haywood

ALCOHOL

Alcohol is an obvious place to start. All cocktails will have a base spirit, and often more than one will be used. To this base spirit, such as vodka, a modifier is added, which works with the base spirit to create a new flavour. Other additions and garnishes can be added which will really bring your base spirit to life.

Cocktails are delicious, and rather enjoyable to consume. However, as the taste of the base spirit is often masked by sweet, strong, or fruity flavours, the true alcohol content of the drink is often deceptive. Remember to pace yourself, sip slowly, and consume water in between cocktails to stay hydrated.

4

B

BLOODY MARY

A Bloody Mary is a classic recipe cocktail, enjoyed by many for decades. Made with tomato juice, vodka, and array of tangy, spicy additions, a Bloody Mary is the perfect way to start a meal.

The Bloody Mary's origin is unclear. Fernand Petiot claimed to have invented the drink in 1921 while working at the New York Bar in Paris, which later became Harry's New York Bar, a frequent Paris hangout for Ernest Hemingway and other American expatriates

Bloody Mary

Ingredients
1 part vodka
4 parts tomato juice
1 dash lemon juice
2 dashes Worcestershire sauce
1 pinch celery salt
Tabasco sauce, to taste
Pepper, to taste

Method
1. In a cocktail shaker, mix all of the ingredients except the Tabasco sauce and pepper.

2. Pour over ice in a goblet.

3. Add Tabasco sauce and pepper to taste, and serve.

6

COCKTAIL

The origin of the word 'cocktail' is often disputed, although many believe the first recorded use of the word cocktail to be from The Morning Post and Gazetteer in London, England in 1798.

Cocktails are often served before dinner, as an aperitif. Other cocktails, such as coffee-based beverages, have been designed to be enjoyed after a meal, or as a nightcap. A 'nightcap' is the colloquial name for a late-night drink, usually the last of the night. A short, strong cocktail is a traditional nightcap,

DARK AND STORMY

Dark and Stormy is a delicious, spicy rum-based cocktail made with dark rum and ginger beer. The Dark and Stormy is the official national drink of Bermuda, where Gosling's Black Seal Rum is made. This classic drink is popular worldwide, especially in many British Commonwealth countries, such as Australia.

Dark and Stormy

Ingredients
2 parts dark rum
4 parts ginger beer
2 lime wedges

Method
1. In a cocktail shaker, mix the rum and ginger beer over ice.

2. Squeeze in one of the lime wedges, and shake again.

3. Pour through a strainer into a highball glass filled with crushed ice, and garnish with lime.

10

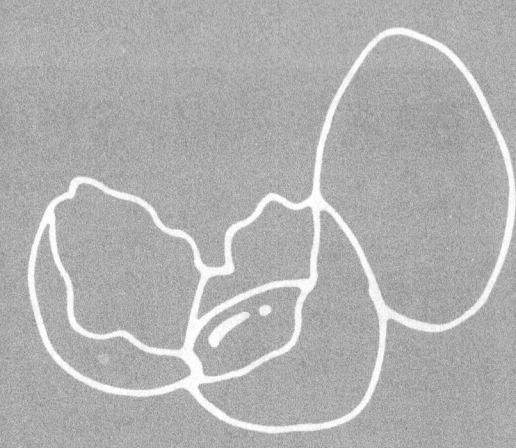

EGGNOG

Eggnog is a popular egg-based cocktail, traditionally enjoyed at Christmas. Using eggs in your cocktail recipes will give your drinks a distinctive taste and texture. There are a number of recipes which call for either eggs, or egg whites, but this is one of the most well known.

Eggnog

Ingredients
1 part brandy
1 part dark rum
1 egg
2 dashes gomme syrup
3 parts milk
Nutmeg, to garnish

Method
1. In a cocktail shaker, mix the brandy, rum, egg and syrup together.

2. Strain into a large tumbler or goblet.

3. Add the milk to the mixture in the glass, and grate a little nutmeg over to garnish.

FRENCH CONNECTION

A French Connection is a delicious cocktail made with Cognac and amaretto. Served in a short tumbler (also called an 'Old Fashioned' glass) a French Connection is a short, strong drink which is perfect as an aperitif.

French Connection

Ingredients
1 part brandy
1 part amaretto

Method
1. In a cocktail shaker, mix the brandy and amaretto.

2. Pour into an ice-filled tumbler.

GLASSWARE

Having a wide range of glassware to serve your carefully prepared cocktails in is important, and the right glass for the right cocktail is as important as any of the ingredients used. There are numerous different types of glasses that you can serve cocktails in, but there are four specific types of glasses that you should try to source first.

The traditional Martini glass is a triangle shaped glass, with a delicate, long stem. A Flute is the type of glass you serve Champagne in. It has a slim glass and a delicate, long stem. A tumbler, also called an Old Fashioned glass, a tumbler is short and sturdy. The highball, also called a long or tall glass, a Highball glass is tall and often slimmer at the bottom than at the top.

HARVEY WALLBANGER

During the 1970s a new wave of cocktails began appearing, and the Harvey Wallbanger was one of them. Simply comprising vodka, Galliano, and orange juice, Harvey Wallbangers are a household favourite, and still enjoyed widely today.

Harvey Wallbanger

Ingredients
1 part vodka
3 parts orange juice
3 dashes Galliano

Method
1. In a cocktail shaker, mix the vodka and the orange juice.

2. Pour into an ice-filled highball glass.

3. Add the dashes of Galliano before serving.

ICE

Ice is an essential addition to many a cocktail. Make sure you have a good supply of ice ready in your freezer before you start mixing your drinks. An ice crusher will also be a good piece of equipment to invest in, although you can improvise if you don't have one; wrap your ice cubes in a clean towel, and using a wide-based bottle or rolling pin, crush the ice and store for use later.

However, not all cocktails will call for crushed ice. The downside of crushed ice is that the smaller pieces of ice will melt more quickly than big cubes. This will dilute your cocktail slightly, and detract from the delicious flavours. Many recipes will simply call for the ingredients to be shaken with ice to make them ice-cold, then strained into an ice-free, chilled glass. Make sure you use the correct type of ice when making cocktails, as it will really make a difference.

JULEP

This cocktail is associated with the Southern states of America, being as it is, based on the traditional Southern spirit, bourbon. Mint, water and sugar are added to make a refreshing drink perfect served with the traditionally spicy foods of the South.

Mint Julep

Ingredients
6-8 leaves fresh mint
1 tbsp sugar
1 tbsp water
1 part bourbon

Method
1. Place 4-5 leaves in a highball glass

2. Sprinkle the sugar and water over the leaves and crush together with a barspoon until the sugar has dissolved.

3. Add the bourbon, and top up with crushed ice.

4. Garnish with the remaining mint before serving.

22

KIR ROYALE

This popular aperitif was originally called blanc-cassis, and was made with Bourgogne Aligoté, a white wine from Burgundy. The drink is now named after Félix Kir who was the mayor of Dijon, in Burgundy. A Kir is made with white wine, but the slightly more special version, the Kir Royale is made with chilled Champagne.

Kir Royale

Ingredients
1 glass chilled Champagne
2 dashes creme de cassis

Method
1. Pour the chilled Champagne into a Champagne flute.

2. Add the cassis and serve.

LONG ISLAND ICE TEA

The Long Island Ice Tea is a cocktail not for the faint hearted. Comprising vodka, gin, tequila, rum, and triple sec, it is rather strong, and deceptively alcoholic. It is thought the Long Island Ice Tea was invented by Robert 'Rosebud' Butt in 1972, as an entry in a contest to create a new mixed drink while he worked at the Oak Beach Inn on Long Island, NY. Try making this delicious drink at home, it is the perfect beverage to get a party started with a bang.

Long Island Ice Tea

Ingredients

1 part vodka
1 part white rum
1 part gin
1 part tequila
1 part triple sec
1 part cola
1 wedge of lime

Method

1. In an ice-filled cocktail shaker mix all of the ingredients together.

2. Pour, through a strainer, into an ice-filled highball glass.

3. Garnish with a wedge of lime before serving.

MARTINI

Possibly the most famous traditional cocktail. The Martini is a cocktail made with gin and vermouth, and garnished with an olive or a lemon twist. Over the years, the Martini has become one of the best-known mixed alcoholic beverages, and can be made in a number of ways, with a variety of ingredients. Try this simple recipe for a classic Dry Martini.

<u>Dry Martini</u>

<u>Ingredients</u>

5 parts gin
1 part dry vermouth
Twist of lemon, to garnish

<u>Method</u>

1. Place the chilled ingredients in a Martini glass.

2. Serve with a twist of lemon.

NEGRONI

The Negroni cocktail is another wonderful aperitif, and can be made with or without soda depending on how strong you like you cocktails to taste. The Negroni was said to be invented in Florence, Italy in 1919, at Caffè Casoni. The drink is still widely enjoyed today.

Negroni

Ingredients
1 part gin
1 part sweet vermouth
1 part Campari
1 part soda water
1 slice of orange

Method
1. Mix the gin, vermouth, and Campari in an ice-filled Old Fashioned glass.

2. Add the soda, and a slice of orange before serving.

30

OLD FASHIONED

Traditionally, the first use of the name 'Old Fashioned' for a bourbon whiskey cocktail was said to have been at the Pendennis Club, a gentlemen's club founded in 1881 in Louisville, Kentucky. The recipe was said to have been invented by a bartender at that club in honor of Colonel James E. Pepper, a prominent bourbon distiller, who brought the cocktail to the Waldorf-Astoria Hotel bar in New York City.

<u>Old Fashioned</u>

<u>Ingredients</u>
2 parts bourbon
2 dashes Angostura bitters
1 part water
1 tsp sugar
1 orange wedge

<u>Method</u>
1. Mix the sugar, water and bitters in an Old Fashioned glass.

2. Add the orange wedge, and muddle with a barspoon.

3. Add the bourbon and a handful of ice cubes and stir before serving.

PINA COLADA

A holiday favourite, and another 1970s classic. On August 16, 1954 at the Caribe Hilton's Beachcomber Bar in San Juan, Puerto Rico the first Piña Colada was mixed by its creator, Ramón Marrero. The Piña Colada has been the official beverage of Puerto Rico since 1978, and is enjoyed around the world to this day. Try making this fruity favourite at home; it is simple, straightforward, and deliciously sweet.

Piña Colada

Ingredients

1 part rum
1 part Malibu
1 part coconut cream
1 part pineapple juice
3-4 pineapple chunks
Maraschino cherry, to garnish

Method

1. In a blender, blitz the rums, coconut cream, pineapple juice and pineapple chunks until smooth.

2. Pour into an ice-filled highball, and add a maraschino cherry to serve.

QUIET SUNDAY

Another simple, sweet and refreshing long cocktail. This cocktail is vodka-based, and the added dashes of Grenadine will give it a beautiful, mottled appearance in the glass. You can experiment with garnishes for this cocktail if you wish, or you can serve it as it is for a really quick and easy summer beverage, perfect for a sunny Sunday.

Quiet Sunday

Ingredients

1 part vodka
4 parts orange juice
3 dashes amaretto
2 dashes Grenadine

Method

1. In a cocktail shaker, mix the vodka, orange juice and amaretto.

2. Pour into an ice-filled highball glass.

3. Add the Grenadine before serving.

RUSTY NAIL

A wonderful, warming cocktail to try at home. This simple recipe for a Rusty Nail is a perfect place to start your cocktail-making journey, and is perfect for whisky-lovers. Carefully scorching the lemon peel for a couple of seconds with a lit match before dropping it into your ice-filled glass will really release the zesty flavours from the rind, leaving a sharp, citrus aroma which will flavour your cocktail to perfection.

Rusty Nail

Ingredients
2 parts Scotch whisky
1 part Drambuie
Twist of lemon peel, to garnish

Method
1. Stir the whisky and Drambuie together in an Old Fashioned glass with a barspoon.

2. Garnish with the lemon peel before serving.

SHAKEN OR STIRRED

To shake, or to stir is a question often asked when discussing the preparation of cocktails. A general rule of thumb is to shake cocktails which include fruit juices, cream liqueurs, syrup, eggs, or dairy products.

Stir cocktails that use distilled spirits or very light mixers only. Stirring is a more gentle technique for mixing cocktails and is a delicate way of combining flavours and ingredients. Many gin and whiskey cocktails, such as Martinis, so as not to 'bruise the gin'.

W. Somerset Maugham declared that "Martinis should always be stirred, not shaken, so that the molecules lie sensuously, one on top of the other." The catchphrase 'shaken not stirred' was made popular by the fictional character, James Bond, who states that his Martinis should be shaken.

TEQUILA SUNRISE

This popular cocktail is another holiday favourite, and is so-called because of the way the ingredients layer themselves in the glass when served. The heavier, denser liquids sink to the bottom and creating a beautiful, blended drink which looks much like a sunset. Tequila Sunrise was originally served at the Arizona Biltmore Hotel, where it was created by Gene Sulit in the 1930s or 1940s. It is still widely made and enjoyed today.

Tequila Sunrise

Ingredients
2 parts tequila
1 part orange juice
2 drops Grenadine

Method
1. In an ice-filled cocktail shaker mix the tequila and orange juice.

2. Pour into a chilled highball glass, and drop in the Grenadine before serving.

UTENSILS

The utensils you will need to make delicious cocktails at home are not difficult to source, and you may find you have many of them already stocked in your kitchen cupboards. It is a good idea to take the time to get your utensils ready before you start mixing cocktails, and having all the tools you need to hand will make your cocktail-making much speedier.

Here is a list of the things you will need to source to begin with. This is, however, a rather basic list and when you have a little experience making cocktails at home you can add to the basics with other fun accessories.

The first piece of equipment you will need is a good cocktail shaker. A shaker with measure marks on the side will be useful, especially if you are a cocktail-making novice! A mixing glass is also important. A mixing glass is a large pint-sized glass, which is often made of thick glass.

A barspoon will also be rather useful to you, to stir, mix and muddle your ingredients in your mixing glass. A barspoon is a small spoon with a long handle, and can be found in most good kitchenware shops.

You may already have a handful of the following pieces of equipment already lurking in kitchen drawers and cupboards. If not, it is a good idea to source a corkscrew, blender, an ice crusher, straws and stirrers.

A strainer is mentioned in many of the recipes in this book, and is imperative when you are shaking your ingredients over ice, but don't want to dilute the drink when it is poured into a glass. Strainers can be found in good kitchenware shops, or you can improvise and pour your mixed drink through a tea strainer and into the serving glass.

VODKATINI

A twist on the classic gin Martini. This cocktail is perfect for vodka-lovers, and you can really get creative with the garnishes that you add. Try a small silverskin onion, or a cocktail olive for a slightly tangy, salty finish to your drink.

Vodkatini

Ingredients
5 parts vodka
1 part dry vermouth
Twist of lemon, to garnish.

Method
1. In an ice-filled cocktail shaker mix the vodka and vermouth.

2. Pour through a strainer into a chilled Martini glass.

3. Add a twist of lemon before serving.

WHITE RUSSIAN

A sweet and creamy cocktail is the perfect alternative to dessert after a meal. The White Russian has been enjoyed for decades, but was made into a household name by the film The Big Lebowski, as the drink of choice of the lead character. You can make an even more indulgent White Russian by adding a little cream to the ingredients before shaking them.

White Russian

Ingredients
2 parts vodka
1 part Khalúa
2 parts milk

Method
1. In an ice-filled cocktail shaker mix the vodka, Khalúa and milk together.

2. Pour through a strainer into a chilled ice-filled highball glass to serve.

XYZ

Another egg-based cocktail, using a hint of the distinctively-flavoured liqueur, Cointreau. If you wanted to add a garnish to this unusual beverage, a piece of orange peel, lightly scorched by a flame would complement the Cointreau perfectly.

XYZ

Ingredients

2 parts rum
1 part Cointreau
1 part lemon juice
1 dash egg white

Method

1. In an ice-filled cocktail shaker mix the ingredients together.

2. Pour through a strainer into a chilled highball glass to serve.

50

YELLOW BIRD

This refreshing and zesty cocktail is the perfect drink to enjoy during the summer. Served in an icy highball glass as a lusciously long beverage it is the perfect drink for a summer's day. Experiment with garnishes for this distinctively-coloured drink, such as a wedge of lime.

Yellow Bird

Ingredients

3 parts white rum
1 part Galliano
1 part Cointreau
1 part fresh lime juice

Method

1. In a cocktail shaker mix the ingredients together.

2. Pour, unstrained, into an ice-filled highball glass

ZOMBIE

This rum-based cocktail is not for the faint hearted! Using three different types of rum, this drink is strong, long, and is given a fresh kick with the mint sprig garnish.

Zombie

Ingredients
2 parts white rum
2 parts dark rum
2 parts golden rum
1 part apricot brandy
1 part lime juice
1 part pineapple juice
1 dash gomme syrup
1 splash Demeraran rum
Sprig of mint (for garnish)

Method
1. Shake all of the ingredients except the Demeraran rum and mint together in a cocktail shaker.

2. Serve in an ice-filled highball glass.

3. Splash in the Demeraran rum before serving, and garnish with a sprig of mint.

TOP TEN TIPS

1. Get all of your utensils and equipment ready before you start mixing your cocktails.

2. Make sure your cocktail shaker is rinsed clean after each drink is mixed.

3. Citrus fruits make a great garnish, but experiment with other fruits to decorate your carefully-created cocktails.

4. Remember to offer your guests a drink of water between each cocktail; the true alcohol content of a cocktail is often hard to gauge as the taste is masked with delicious fruit juices and mixers!

5. Try storing your glasses in a freezer before use, for a fantastic frosted finish on your glassware.

6. Hunt in charity shops and thrift stores for traditional cocktail glasses, you might get lucky and find some great pieces.

AND TRICKS

7. Substituting the alcohol in your cocktails for fruit juices and cordials is a great way to make an alcohol-free beverage that can be enjoyed by all.

8. Keep an eye out for fun stirrers and straws when you enjoy drinks at a cocktail bar. They can be recycled and used at home to give your homemade cocktails a professional touch.

9. You can get really creative and make your own home-made liqueurs to use in your cocktail making.

10. Making and designing your own cocktails is the perfect way to mark a special occasion, such as a birthday or engagement. You can even give the cocktail a special name, and make your celebration extra memorable.

Two Magpies

Copyright © 2013 Two Magpies Publishing
An imprint of Read Publishing Ltd
Home Farm, 44 Evesham Road, Cookhill, Alcester,
Warwickshire, B49 5LJ

Commissioning Editor Rose Hewlett
Words by Sophie Berry
Design and Illustrations by Zoë Horn Haywood

This book is copyright and may not be reproduced or copied in any way without the express permission of the publisher in writing.

British Library Cataloguing-in-Publication Data A catalogue record for this book is available from the British Library.